Copyright © 2020 by Khadizhat Witt

All rights reserved. No part of this publication may be reproduced, distributed, or transmitted in any form or by any means, including photocopying, recording, or other electronic or mechanical methods without the prior written permission of the author, except in the case of brief quotations embodied in critical reviews and certain other noncommercial uses permitted by copyright law. For permission requests, contact the author at the email below.

circumwanderers@gmail.com

This book is dedicated to my daughter Aya who started traveling the world when she was 6 weeks old, and to my husband Justin who makes these travels possible.

Nick, Aya and their parents, Kate and George, leave Los Angeles and eight hours later land in Lima, Peru. Can you guess where father George has a scientific assignment this time? Keep reading, and you will find out.

The first day starts at the Historic Center of Lima, where they pass by the Government Palace, which is the official residence of the President of Peru. While Nick is observing the officers standing outside of the Palace, Aya is looking around and pointing at the Basilica Cathedral of Lima and exclaims, "Daddy, look, the crosses on the roof of that building are just like the crosses we saw on the church in Russia! Is this also a church?"

"It is a Roman Catholic Cathedral," her father explains. "This building where people pray also represents Christianity, just a little differently from what we had seen in Russia. Would you like to go inside?"

After the Cathedral, the family has dinner at a local restaurant in the district of Miraflores. They try a QUINOA soup and a Peruvian CEVICHE, which is a dish made of fish, potatoes, corn, onions, lemon and lime juices, and herbs.

"Mom, you mentioned that we would see earth drawings including long lines which can be seen all the way from space. What are they?" wonders Nick.
"The Nazca Lines are large designs of various shapes which were made on the ground by people who lived here long before us. They are surprisingly precise, considering that those who made them could never see them from above like we do now!" George explains.

The next day, the family takes a short flight to Iquitos, a city that can only be reached by plane or by boat. During the flight, they pass by the Andes Mountains and then the rainforest. When Nick sees a river winding its way through the jungle he asks, "Dad, is this the famous Amazon River?"

"We are looking at the Ucayali River which is one of the headwaters of the Amazon," responds George.

"There are so many trees… it looks like a rainforest I saw in one of my books," adds Aya.

The travelers get accommodated at the lodge on the bank of the Amazon River. Aya can't wait to explore the wildlife and pleads, "Mom, when are we going to see the monkeys and big swimming cows? I forgot what those are called."

Nick shares her impatient excitement, adding, "And pink dolphins, too?"

They board a small wooden boat with a motor and soon arrive at a place called Monkey Island.
"Can I hold one of them?" asks Aya. "They are so cute!"
Soon she is happily cradling a baby monkey in her arms. After that the family goes on to watch pink dolphins.

"Mom, why are these dolphins pink? They are usually gray, aren't they?" wonders Nick.

"Some believe the dolphins that live in parts of the Amazon evolved to be pink because they match the colors of reddish mud that occurs in the rivers after rains. But there are many other guesses about this subject," explains Kate.

"Tomorrow I am meeting with my colleagues and we are going to the jungle with a local guide. Who wants to join me?" asks George.

"I would like to go with you, Dad! I really enjoyed observing your studies in Kamchatka when we were in Russia. I learned a lot about the wildlife there. I want to see what creatures live here," responds Nick.

"And what about me? What am I going to do?" asks Aya.

"If you want, dear, we can visit a Wildlife Rescue Center and Sanctuary, and won't need to walk as far as your brother and father," offers Kate.

Aya gladly agrees and the following day she is learning about animals and birds she had seen before only in books and cartoons. "Look mom! This is Macaw and a Blue Morpho Butterfly!"

"Is this a real jaguar?"
"Yes it is! And look, over there is a manatee, the creature you called a big swimming cow," Kate smiles, pointing at one of the pools of water.

"This is an Arapaima, also known as Paiche, a large predatory fish that lives in some of the rivers of the rainforest," explains mom to her daughter.

Meanwhile, Nick and his father, together with other scientists, walk through the jungle and record their findings about various plants. On their path, they meet a large poisonous spider called a Tarantula, and an Anaconda, the world's largest snake.

"Look at this vine! It looks just like a snake. I feel like it's talking to me," says Nick.
"It might be! This plant is called Ayahuasca, and is used by traditional medicine men for healing those people who want its help," comments the local guide.

From the hot and humid Amazon basin
the family flies to the town of Cusco,
located high in the Andes Mountains.

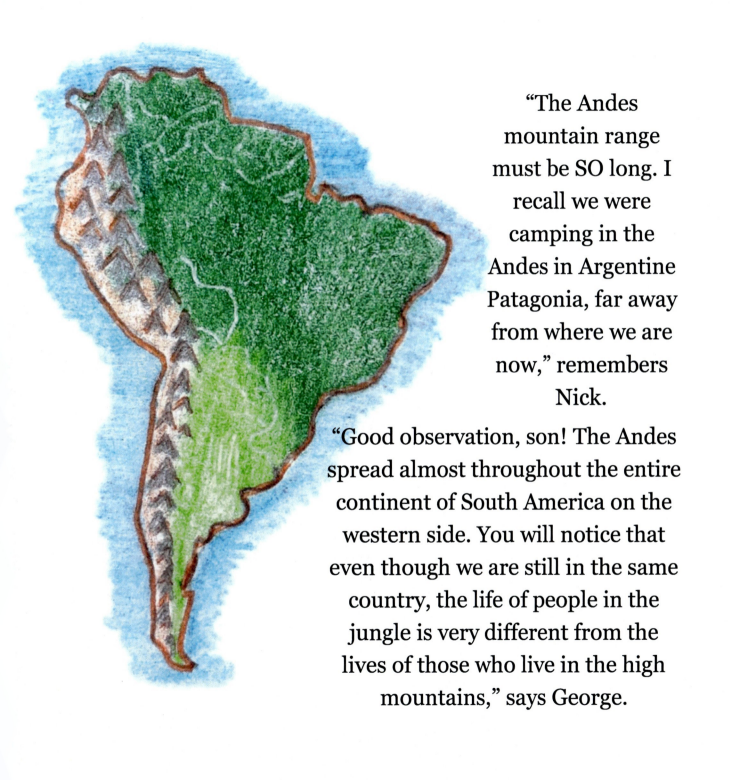

"The Andes mountain range must be SO long. I recall we were camping in the Andes in Argentine Patagonia, far away from where we are now," remembers Nick.

"Good observation, son! The Andes spread almost throughout the entire continent of South America on the western side. You will notice that even though we are still in the same country, the life of people in the jungle is very different from the lives of those who live in the high mountains," says George.

Together again, the family travels to Machu Picchu and after a long trek they reach a very tall mountain with old ruins on its top.

"I am looking at the maze. It's like a labyrinth. Look at those rooms and house-like structures!" exclaims Nick.

Before Nick finishes his sentence, Aya takes off running through the maze yelling, "Catch me" to her brother. When her parents and Nick catch up to her, Aya asks, "Who built all this?"

"It is believed that people of the Inca Empire constructed this during the 15th century," her father answers.

On their way from Machu Picchu they pass by another river running between tall mountains.
Kate explains to her kids, "This valley through which Urubamba River flows, long ago, was the center of Inca Civilization. People here grow crops like quinoa, corn, and over 3000 types of potatoes."
"3000! That is a lot! I have only seen 4 in our grocery store," concludes Aya.

"Look at that lady carrying a child on her back!" Nick points out the window of the tour bus as they drive through the town of Maras. "Her clothes are so beautiful, bright and colorful," Aya observes. "I want a dress like that too."

"And what are those?" asks Nick. They all look to see square and rectangular pools that range from white to reddish to brown in color.

George explains, "These are salt evaporation ponds. The saline water gets into them from underground streams, then it dries in the pond and then people come and gather salt from it."

"And when they finish, the water fills the ponds again?" wonders Nick.

"Exactly right!" confirms Kate.

From Cusco the family goes to Puno, a town on the shore of Lake Titicaca, the largest lake on the entire continent of South America. They want to see floating islands inhabited by indigenous people.

"How do the islands float?!" questions Nick.

"They are made of a tall plant called TOTORA REED which grows on the edges of the lake. From this plant, local people make huts, furniture, canoe-shaped boats and the foundation floor of the island itself," explains George to his children.

"But how do they watch TV?" wonders Aya.

"They don't have televisions," Kate reminds them. "They don't have access to many things that we have, but they live closer to nature and that is to their advantage. One day you will probably understand that nature gives us everything we actually need, and we just need to appreciate and preserve those precious gifts."

During the flight from Lima to Los Angeles, both Nick and Aya are thinking about the gifts that Mother Nature shares with all of us. And you? Can you tell your parents or grandparents or aunts and uncles what you receive from nature every day?

Made in the USA
Las Vegas, NV
14 May 2023